better together*

*This book is best read together, grownup and kid.

 akidsco.com

a kids book about

a kids book about FOOD ALLERGIES

by Ina K. Chung

a kids book about

Text and design copyright © 2023
by A Kids Book About, Inc.

Copyright is good! It ensures that work like this can exist, and more work in the future can be created.

All rights reserved. No part of this publication may be reproduced, distributed, or transmitted in any form or by any means, including photocopying, recording, other electronic or mechanical methods, without the prior written permission of the publisher, except in the case of brief quotations embodied in critical reviews and certain other noncommercial uses permitted by copyright law. For permission requests, write to the publisher.

A Kids Book About, Kids Are Ready, and the colophon 'a' are trademarks of A Kids Book About, Inc.

Printed in the United States of America.

A Kids Book About books are available online: *akidsco.com*

To share your stories, ask questions, or inquire about bulk purchases (schools, libraries, and nonprofits), please use the following email address: *hello@akidsco.com*

Print ISBN: 979-8-89281-006-7
Ebook ISBN: 979-8-89281-007-4

Designed by Rick DeLucco
Edited by Emma Wolf

To my children, who have turned me into the advocate I never thought I could become. My dream for you both is that the world will accept you and celebrate you like I do. You belong.

INTRO

Do you know someone with food allergies? If you don't yet, you probably will. And even though there are many people with food allergies these days, there is still a lot that people don't understand about them. To be honest, even I can't fully understand what it's like, and I have to trust what my daughter tells me about her own experience.

Food allergies can feel scary and isolating, but the more people learn about them, the more others can understand what it takes to keep kids with food allergies safe. And the better we all are for it.

HI THERE.

MY NAME IS INA.

I don't have any food allergies, but my daughter is allergic to…

Do you know what food allergies are?

A FOOD ALLERGY happens when the body's immune system identifies specific foods as harmful and reacts by causing symptoms.

This is called an allergic reaction, which can range from being uncomfortable to deadly.

Some examples of symptoms include:

- **ITCHY HIVES**
- **VOMITING**
- **TROUBLE BREATHING**
- **SWELLING**
- **DIARRHEA**
- **(AND OTHERS)**

That sounds scary, right?

IT CAN BE.

But there are many medications that can help reverse these symptoms and make someone with an allergy feel better.

Some people experience **AN INTOLERANCE TO PARTICULAR FOODS,** which means their body has a harder time processing those foods.

People with either an intolerance or allergy may experience discomfort with certain foods.

But with allergies, that discomfort can qu

ANAPH

ckly become a life-threatening event, called

YLAXIS.

And for some people, anaphylaxis can happen immediately and can mean

INCREASED HEART RATE, VOMITING, SWELLING, OR DIZZINESS.

Avoiding situations that cause anaphylaxis is a crucial part of each day when you have a food allergy.

SO, WHAT DOES A DAY-TO-DAY ROUTINE LOOK LIKE FOR PEOPLE WITH FOOD ALLERGIES?

I READ EVERY **FOOD LABEL** TO MAKE SURE MY DAUGHTER'S FOOD IS FREE OF HER ALLERGENS.

I TALK WITH HER **TEACHERS** AT THE START OF EVERY YEAR TO MAKE SURE THEY KNOW HOW TO KEEP HER SAFE.

I CALL **RESTAURANTS** IN ADVANCE TO FIND OUT WHETHER THEY CAN ACCOMMODATE HER ALLERGIES.

EVERY PLAY DATE, EVERY BIRTHDAY PARTY, EVERY SLEEPOVER, WE TALK ABOUT WHAT FOODS WILL BE SERVED AND WHETHER SHE NEEDS TO BRING AN ALTERNATIVE.

WE WASH HANDS WITH SOAP AND WATER OFTEN, AND I ASK OTHERS TO WASH THEIR HANDS JUST IN CASE THEY'VE HANDLED HER ALLERGENS.

I ALWAYS HAVE HER EPINEPHRINE* WITH ME, AND WE BRING EPINEPHRINE WHEREVER SHE GOES.

*Epinephrine is a medication that can reverse the effects of anaphylaxis. An epinephrine auto-injector is inserted into the thigh muscle like a shot, and anyone can help if they know how to use it.

This is what a day looks like with *my* kid, but all food allergies are different.

Everyone has different needs and different levels of sensitivity.

FOR EXAMPLE, many people can't have foods that have even come into contact with one of their allergens.

This is called...

Let's say you go to a sandwich shop and order one without cheese because of an allergy to it.

FOR SOME PEOPLE, if the employee uses a knife that sliced cheese earlier that day, and then uses it on their sandwich, they may still have an allergic reaction.

The cheese itself doesn't even have to be near it!

IT CAN BE TH

AT SERIOUS.

Food allergies are
a lot to think about.

And it can feel like they're
outside of one's control.

But with

PRACTICE, PATIENCE, AND COMMUNITY SUPPORT,*

managing them is possible.

*Providing support to a food allergy family
can be as easy as asking a simple question:
"How can we make this environment safe for you?"

Here's the most important thing
I want kids with food allergies to know:

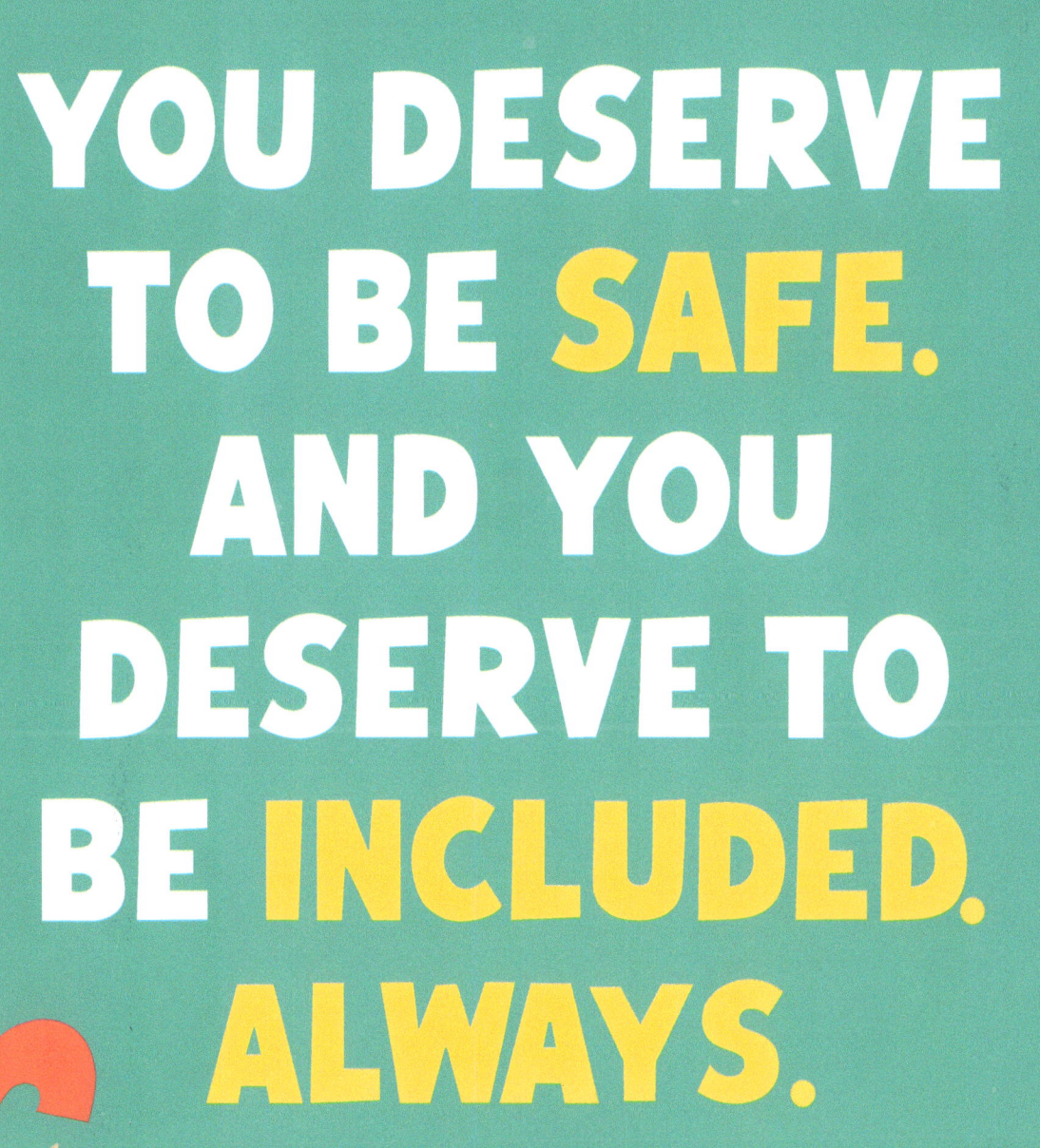

AND YOU DESERVE TO HAVE

CARE A LOT ABOUT Y

PEOPLE AROUND YOU WHO
OU AND YOUR SAFETY.

You didn't choose
to have this condition.

AND I KNOW IT CAN BE FRUSTRATING.

But you have the right to advocate for yourself and make sure you get what you need.

I hope you'll share whatever you feel with grownups and friends you trust.

You are allowed to feel frustrated, or disappointed,

BUT YOU ARE NEVER ALONE.

THERE'S A LOT TO LEARN ABOUT YOUR ALLERGIES.

And as you learn more, you'll be able to make decisions that are right for you.

Even if others don't fully understand, trust what you know about yourself.

I want a world where my daughter and kids like you can **ENJOY THEIR LIVES WITHOUT FEAR OR EXCLUSION.**

A world where their allergies aren't treated as an inconvenience (because they aren't).

Where everyone learns to ask good questions and is willing to learn.

AND WHERE EVE
SAFE AND LIKE

RYONE CAN FEEL
THEY BELONG.

OUTRO

I'm so grateful you're reading this book. And I know many families that manage food allergies will want me to include (and dispel) some of the big myths about food allergies, because there are a lot! Can we dive in?

A tiny bit of a food allergen won't hurt... right? It can.

An allergic reaction is only serious if the person can't breathe, right? Nope. Please look up "anaphylaxis" for more details.

Gluten-free food is safe for people with food allergies, right? Gluten-free food is free of gluten but can still contain any number of allergens.

Nuts are the most dangerous food allergy, aren't they? Any food allergen can cause a life-threatening reaction, and all food allergies should be taken seriously.

And there are so many more. Please visit **Food Allergy Research & Education** at **foodallergy.org** for more information.

About The Author

As a Korean American mom to a kid with food allergies, Ina is passionate about sharing the food of her heritage with families who experience food allergies. She was surprised to learn that many people avoid all Asian food, or are fearful of it, due to food allergies. Ina wants people to know that the thousands of amazing dishes and dozens of cuisines that make up Asian food are incredibly diverse and can be quite allergy-friendly—yes, even for peanut, egg, or sesame allergies!

Kids with food allergies deserve everything their friends deserve: tasty food, safety, and feeling like they belong. Ina hopes for a future for kids with food allergies that is safe, delicious, and inclusive.

 @theasianallergymom   theasianallergymom.com

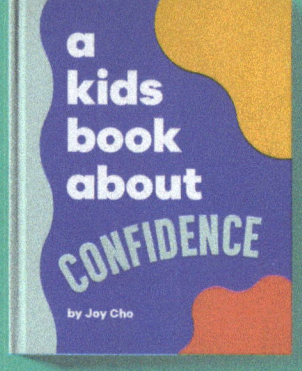
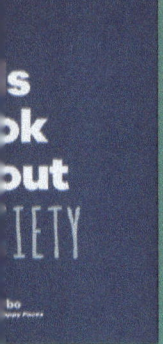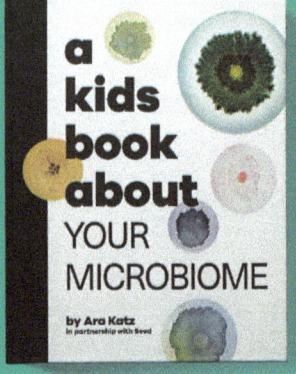

Discover more at akidsco.com

www.ingramcontent.com/pod-product-compliance
Lightning Source LLC
Chambersburg PA
CBHW061359010526
44107CB00012B/985